Looking for Disappearance

poems by

Karen Arnold

Finishing Line Press
Georgetown, Kentucky

Looking for Disappearance

Copyright © 2023 by Karen Arnold
ISBN 979-8-88838-187-8 First Edition
All rights reserved under International and Pan-American Copyright Conventions. No part of this book may be reproduced in any manner whatsoever without written permission from the publisher, except in the case of brief quotations embodied in critical articles and reviews.

ACKNOWLEDGMENTS

"Kennebec" *Kerf* 2022 edition
"Inside/Outside" *Carmina*, March 2022
"Winter Eclipse" *Vesper* I Fall/Winter 2021
"Astronomy" *Gyroscope* September 2020, reprint *Carmina* September 2021
"Hours on the Shore" *Connecticut Review* June 2020
"Passing Time" *Pinyon Spring* 2020
"Sleep" *Front Range Review* Spring 2020
"Night Driving" *Scarlet Leaf Review* October 2019
"What keeps us" *Slant* Spring 2019 revised and titled "Conundrum"

Publisher: Leah Huete de Maines
Editor: Christen Kincaid
Cover Art: Jan Rickman
Author Photo: Jan Rickman
Cover Design: Elizabeth Maines McCleavy

Order online: www.finishinglinepress.com
also available on amazon.com

Author inquiries and mail orders:
Finishing Line Press
PO Box 1626
Georgetown, Kentucky 40324
USA

Table of Contents

Winter Eclipse 1

Omen 2

Inside/Outside 3

Astronomy 4

Without 5

Handpainting 7

Passing Time 8

About Flight 9

Night Driving 11

Anemia/Taking the Waters 14

Nightsong 15

Conundrum 16

Kennebec 17

Plunder.. 18

Monet in Time 21

Among Monet's Canvases 23

Hours on the Shore 27

Winter Eclipse

I

More sloppily than in the way of phases
the moon begins to disappear—
Clouds shape and blow past her like snow that forgot to fall
She shines wide—a smoke of shadow
        flickering ahead of the dark,
                moving slowly despite Earth's surface winds
                        gusting snow off porches, powdered stars

Above us she waits to be eclipsed
I call my daughters
want to know if they see the ripe Renaissance moon
        corpulent, inconstant
                or darkling prophecies—visions
                        of past mythologies at the frigid hour
I wonder if my friend on far Trondheim's fjord
sees Diana surrender to a shadow incandescent as fire
one we both know to be earth—cold and hard under us
I want to call my mother—whose spirit escaped last September
        rising to the white light of infinity this disc only mimics

tell her to step out on her Chicago balcony
                try to find the renegade moon
who has done nothing but repeat her rounds—
                      now vanishing
        the way she did in her hospital bed
            appearing to be still
                a familiar face
                    echoing our past
                          containing our rituals
as the moon affirms Earth's path
                        by her vanishing act

Omen

II

Impatient for some
hint of motion
I leave and enter
the house repeatedly

swathed in scarves and jackets
confused by a collage
of images—Persephone
                    at cliff's edge
waves white beneath her
Isis watching
                    sand slide
over the night desert

Isolate
on the short front walk
I wait for
        a visitation
                    moment — holy
unhampered

by snow plows scraping
or airplanes
        counterfeit stars

                        some flickering light
                            that very message from

the conjuring moon
that myth and rebirth attend
our remaking

under the orange gypsy dance
of scarves and firelight
fomenting her eclipse

Inside/Outside

III

The moon goes murky
my darkened kitchen
smells of peppermint tea
Alice in Wonderland—Our Lady of the Lake
collect around me
under the apricot smudge
that lately lit porch chairs
blue under carapace tarps

In this odd dark
a copper deck chime
calls the Lady of Avalon's acolytes
to Druid rites on nights
colder than this minus 6 degree wind chill

Wind, strange sister seeking asylum,
wraps me with a care for night travel
I press my cheek to the cold window
watch the moon swim
backward from light

Astronomy

This month Venus, 1.5 million miles from Earth
rises at sunset—lingers just above the horizon
    flirting with us where we shop
        work, carry on our coupling
It may trick us glimmering in haze and reflections
        glancing off dust our lives agitate on the planet
be mistaken for a plane, lining up for touch down
        flashing mixed messages in the nearly-night sky

Venus hovers beyond comprehension—
    love planet visible just a few half-bright hours
        summons a half-draped, armless, marble nude
          turned slightly toward a barely audible call—
low in the sky
        gone by the time night floods rising space
          with gleams that signal distance
Venus, barely marking the March sky
    your habits, your appearance, your allure elude me,
      anchored to a close by site, small planet
          set low in my body
a landscape not quite 1.5 million miles from my center
    whose rising has shifted to a shadow
        hovers in the lives of my daughters
an all but forgotten presence
    overshadowed by distance   marks the border of my next
        season
    in tides of energy and moon spells

Without

my mother's sleep
                wrapped around

the memory of
our lives
                days she felt me—
                strange disturbance—
                set in motion by
                my father's uniformed presence
squalling out
as he learned to fly
        I can't rest

My days break
unremarked
by her breaths
regular
as currents
pattern rivers
                She no longer
                holds me

        somewhere

hoards me deep—
a squinting six-year-old
she saved with glasses—
                awkward—
                taller than everyone

sees me
in a pool of light
reading
oblivious to her calls

                    I toss in dark
                    mourn
                    mornings she brushed
                    fist-tight curls
                    me howling, indignant

          The wind seems lonely

Night's restless dreams
sift girlhood's sidewalks—
where she watched skating,
bike riding, whooping
                    summer days
                    out of sequence
                    her face nowhere—
                    her vision
                    of our brick Cape Cod
                    erased by disappearance
          Sleep
confuses time and people

Lives tumble oddly
old schoolrooms and my children
dinner tables and two lane roads
a welter of cross-references   my mother's sighs
                                        or laughing
          carried from her war years

keep me four—
helping her wash the floor
in our Polk Street
Chicago
apartment
                              She and I
                              in sloshing water
          sharing her work

Handpainting

I recall my mother
polishing her nails
white half moons
scalloped
over the base of each
She pulled deftly
a perfect arc

her drawing hand
balanced on her pinky
the same way
she steadied a brush
over china plates
painting ivy
before baking them

The rising moon
still leaves—tang of paint
captured me—
till she stopped
year uncertain
but not the obvious
attention to
                detail

Passing Time

Riding west
Youngstown to Gary
one Crayola-red truck
gleaming beside a house
snaps my father back
our history just beginning
He's twenty in the picture—
leg cocked up on the truck step
elbow balanced there
a Camel dangling from his fingers
he flashes sex
cock-sure
in his leather jacket
The arrogance of pilots and men
lifts off the print—
"SOUTHERN EXPRESS"
arcs across the cab door
cold leather seats behind it
maps and shift sticks
all he needs for freedom and the road
After the war he rode
the restlessness of flight
hauling steel
posing for my mother in the snow
laughing
just enough
to catch me driving by
thirty years after his death

About Flight

      I

Naked
compelled
to catch them
at windows
in high disarray
but
steady in motion

I clutched at
white curtains
they clatter-called
codes
unclear to me
except
for my knowing
their near-barks
marked spring—
the syntax of
moving

shivering, watching
ignoring the cold
hearing geese follow
maps
only they fathom

      ll

The wisdom of pilots
steel wings and vibration
must feel like
instinct

after awhile
For me
it was breathless
My father
flew
over roads
we had driven
just minutes before

The secret of motion
kept us aloft
stolen from birds
a part of the sky
swept across
fields and creeks
before landing
sun-strapped and panting
our hearts
in the clouds

        III

Grounded
still sensing
the dance
of geese riding
their gypsy migration
slicing through sky
I turned to
return to my
man
balanced lightly
caught in the motion
toward mating and chance

Night Driving

I

Concrete sluices underneath
but the Platte rises in my mind
a river I have never seen surfaces
    the sound of wheels
      squeaking west
      shouts of children
      begging to ride or walk
      women jounced on wagon seats
      the tiresome, stinking work of walking alongside animals
billows into consciousness
as I work north to
Maine-air nights where
windows bedside slice
cold against the cheek

I go to water winding up the Kennebec to Bath
    and back to sea
      a steady whispered slide
      a rattling white roil as
      tide reverses
      indifferent slaps in slight wind
      or lapping wash in wakes of motors
water known by sound

The unknown Platte haunts
    its sand bar fords
      the shush of grasses—wind or water blown
      wind-chopped shallow sweeps
insinuate themselves
I hurtle through night towns
Lowell, Lawrence on the Merrimac
that swept away the lives of women
weaving

swept them into wilderness
dark nights, fatigued—the same as
wagons echoing my Platte drudged west

   I push north
   in quest of silence
   rocks, the unforgiving
   heaving, little-caring ocean
        poise myself
          and gamble possibilities
          on planes that carry ships and light
          on to beyond
weigh my significance
as ever-winding spools of tide slip up rocks
cut water's high mark, blackened rim

II

     Life on the trail
     the gypsy swell of grasses over nomads
     that life I do not own
     but flight I know
     the half mad sense
     of tramping out
     to shed dark struggles
     half-done deeds
     abandoned
     for coastal lights
     flashing near me
     island to island, shore to point
     cove's end to ledge's

I am my dark pilgrim self
exhausted
flung into the river
following the course it carves
across the land
to shores
where life resumes
on terms set
by the roar of wind
currents off rocky ledges
faith in the urge to flee

Anemia/Taking the Waters

could not run
dreamt of my children dying
          did not care
                    exhaustion outlasting sleep

voice dried
hair went straight
that year my blood went white
                              We drove north

In a Maine cottage
I stopped listening to blood
              rush in my ears
longed for rest
sat before a birch fire
        glad to have no lights
                push darkness further off—

                        stood on a midnight porch
                        listening to the train of the sea
                        a quarter mile away, always
                              coming home
                              sounds of migration
fed on repetition
        tides stumbling in and out
                    over stone footings

In the grey cottage
        staring late into embers
                waiting for light to die
                        grateful for slow burning elms—

blood
        rising with tides
                deepening Back Cove's end

Nightsong

Alone on the small porch
I surrender to currents
waves of wind slap leaves
imagine Ophelia
fearing an uncertain future

Back Cove's water
captures an ivory moon
signals that
even the child at my breast
and contemplation

will not be enough
to keep me from riding
the wind of dark tides
keep me from sinking
my heart in the nest

Conundrum

Perched on the edge
listening to surf slush and run
over rocks—tides coming in
pull us nightly
to Pemaquid's sun
orange, fierce pink, pale yellow
beyond the dark point

Landlocked
we read—content
almost indifferent—
reach lazily for wine coolers
as if we had no place to go
as if July had another two months

When a full moon
summons
we stand
at the wide kitchen door
leaning
listening to crickets—night birds
expansive light fills us

After digging the garden
smelling old moisture
planting ageratum, begonias, basil
we water, smugly
confident
flowers will come without
ceremonies danced
pollen tossed to the wind

The curse of the darling cosmos
seduces us
quiet or wild
beside turned earth
fecund, strong, elusive
moving just beyond
the known

Kennebec

At least twice daily
the river talks to itself
here where it flows
round Fiddler's Reach—
with shuffling—

faking
a small boat's wake
on an otherwise
silent afternoon
where even leaffall startles

No breeze quivers
Birds have ceased
flight and sound
except the eagle

a white tipped slash
keeping the shore
beyond old pines
some dead, all wind-warped

Any summer day
the bubbling watery confusion
would lose to shouts
bird calls, lawn mowers ashore

but today—
Earth's tide
takes silence victim
whispers as it
turns decidedly
upriver

Plunder

I

Colorado the first sacrifice
hot summer simmers
in mid-Atlantic states
Years of needles and leaves carpet
stands of timber
unprotected
even by that huge water
Tinder waits
for lightning
an errant spark

New England's fire signs
read high for probability
Grasses sun-scorched
groves brown
wait
where floods have not ravaged
Southern corn or cotton

Our lives seem inviolate
hedged by roads
malls, hospitals
occasional swaths of green
Facing ferocity
we plan
to flee by car
ride rivers
cutting through cities

Old habits—
seeking higher ground
to outwit floods
or cellars
if tornados rage
to counter danger—
won't slow rampage
in the face of fire

II

Rocks, shells
volcanic tempered
sea glass
may survive
I crave driftwood
shore-hoarded
from ledges, beaches
jumbled with
bladderwack and broken reeds
flung from the sea
still fat with smell of salt—
want it with me—
against reason

III

A lust for
plunder from the deep
seems odd
to those unused to waves—
not greedy for the force of
wind against the point—
where ragged shore grass
shivers in the wind
or storms beach
long-dead trees—
where seals mate close in and
cormorants seem living cuts
of darkness between waves

Such lust fills hands
with shells, rocks, driftwood
pictures
a wedding ring
and one gold chain

Monet in Time
    Chicago 1995

Ragged muffins of wheat stacks
    mists above the Seine
        Camille's cloudy death mask
            accumulated struggles abandoned

River-like—a ragged current
    shifts   slip of perception
        reflection
casting back glances   our comprehension
        creates a paradox in three dimensions
seeing sight   reflected being seen

The gallery fills—
    sight and scene reverse
angles of perception
        eyes click constantly
                intimate cessations
        take in transformations
             mysteries of refraction

Outside three arched windows Chicago drives by
    Jackson bridges tracks
        a park greens between Michigan and Columbus
            hung under grey-white quiet afternoon
                inside high windowed alcoves

Squat iron refuse cans
    square lampposts marking space and light
        gas lamps and discs score La Gare Saint-Lazar
One bridge further
        Victorian streetlamps mirror Monet
    yellow canna, red flecked
            mimic Giverny

Lily ponds
        confusing   sky water cloud
                              free form figures
            ghost white shapes
                                    turquoise—lavender

We gather silent
           between murals, final walls of eyes and light
           fevered
                strokes

cas
  ca
    ding   to fend off   lost
                                        illumi
                                            nation
                arcs
            a luminous bridge between
the light   the eye   the viewer
              elevation

Among Monet's Canvases

I

Somehow
      the clock of wheatstacks or fields
          the pendulum of tides and coastal hours
              calls up daughters
                      lives in motion
Monet would love the incongruity
      French light and focus engendering
          American girls
              brash, political, vulnerable,
                      distinctly themselves

II

Obsessed by the press of the personal
      he turned his eye on landscapes
          immune to the cliche of the familiar
filled canvases with
      Camille, the turn of her head
              Jean asleep
                  a garden stroll
Light sang, slashed to brilliance
      in fields of vision
          here a green umbrella
              strewn—spine and handle up
                near Camille—seated
                    wind caught in trees listing left
                          the slip of breeze

    in skirts and veils   Bezon's cocked parasol   teased by easy gusts

Heat second to movement
                    air
                              bright flood of sun

III

Taken in with sympathy, companionable grace
    I catch the reflex, tic toward languor
        known from childhood on
            shade falling from slim trunks in dark grass stripes
              cut by blue, green, chunks of white
                    laid on with palette knife, blunt brush

IV

By sleight of shifting light
        Camille on an elbow
            yellow light, a glow
                conjures daughters'
                      lives strung casually over years

common figures made uncommon
        like her veil and summer clouds flowing, captured
            as if their movements in my life would never cease—
                our domestic entourage sun splashed

V

Sensing fleeting mother-me
        measuring
            passages outside windows, over beaches
                          parking lot tarmac
movement past me
    toward
        away
            the wind of lifting off
                      the youngest girl's flight
                              reveled in

VI

Galleries close me in the moment
        light cast
              through tides of silence
                              from old stars
casts me back
        to mother/daughter boundaries once familiar

VII

Rooms near
        my Chicago childhood
                evoke uncertainty
                      shift to another plane
Poised
        questioning   I pass
                Monet's canvases
                my histories
                      women-daughters
                              muse
Will we agree after all
        on how the light fell
                or if keeping it is good?

VIII

I slip further back
    Images of my grandmother's departures and homecomings mingle
        Monet's mystery of color and clouds
            anchored to landscape
                intensify with thoughts of Lily
                      on the surface of my first Swedish day

      free-floating
  the way a drop of water enters a stream
  my own brand of immigrant
  packing a child's memories

                    searching for unknown sources
                    my past in a country's name

IX

I meet Monet
      where sight, perception
                quicken…avalanche

Daughters surface continually
      their odd attendance unbidden
I cannot halt convergence
      images
          the drowse of wind
                the pressure of time

Hours on the Shore
    The Art Institute, Chicago

Monet's blues and violets fill my mind
    his last great sweep of murals
        gives up lilies and light
            shapes slung
                in long strokes
                    cathedral-like against white walls

They hang the world, fading
    last light measured
        as sight dissolved—
            into an odd amalgam of cataracts
                that efflorescence the man labored
                to lay down
                    in paint from his first day of work

In cool space
  sited in semi-darkness
    the gleam of gold screens—old Japan reflecting
      thinly from the deep wood floor
            locus between meridians

a third point floating
    between galleries and desire
        mesmerized by the variety
            light detonates over water

                the master's vibrant seas of light
                    his life's work
                        our daughters
set out like lilies
  seen in every imaginable light
    surrendered to public places
        figures in a world of violent hungers
            blooming life's yes—grow on
                roots and rooms and wombs
                    belonging only to themselves

Gardens of light
    float and flower
        seasons filtered through new-old eyes
            women
                listening to sighs
                    of wind across water
                        the swing of their bodies
                            spiraling in a woman's way
                                seeding, blooming, shadowing
                                landscapes
                                    cut with furrows
                                        of their own

Karen Arnold, literary gypsy, independent scholar and writer, has facilitated Maryland Humanities, local library and NEH funded reading and discussion series throughout Maryland for over thirty years. She has taught at the University of Lund in Sweden; the United States Naval Academy, where she also directed two plays; and the University of Maryland College Park. She was Poet-in-Residence at Montpelier Cultural Arts Center in Laurel, MD where she taught creative writing and autobiography workshops and organized a poetry reading series. She has taught in the Johns Hopkins University Osher Adult Education programs and has created and facilitated Maryland Humanities Literature and Medicine discussion series at Baltimore hospitals and now does the same for Veterans in Baltimore area libraries and cultural arts centers. Her book, *Border Crossings,* appeared in 1997. Her work can be found in *Trajectory, Slant, Pinyon, Front Range Review, Carmina, Little Patuxent Review, Evening Street Press* and other journals. She got her masters and PhD at the University of Maryland where she worked with former US Poet Laureate Reed Whittemore, was Assistant Director of Freshman Composition, and a master teacher. Midwestern wide skies and openness spawned her love of Atlantic shores.

www.ingramcontent.com/pod-product-compliance
Lightning Source LLC
Chambersburg PA
CBHW022127090426
42743CB00008B/1041